The CENTRAL STEWARTI

by
Jack Hunter

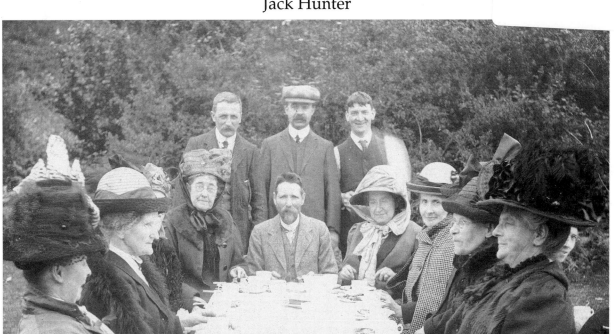

Members of a picnic party stoically prepare to eat an alfresco meal at Kirkdale Port, situated where the Kirkdale Burn runs into Wigtown Bay. Kirkdale Port was a favourite destination for both institutional and informal outings, especially from Newton Stewart. In spite of its name, it never seems to have been a recognised landing place, not surprisingly given the inhospitable nature of the foreshore. However, in the mid-nineteenth century it was for a time a fishing station. It seems likely that it was used in the late eighteenth and early nineteenth centuries by smugglers, for a number of reputed smugglers' caves are to be found in the vicinity.

Kirkpatrick Gatehouse - of - Fleet. N.B.

ACKNOWLEDGEMENTS

I have to thank the following people for information generously given: Mr H. McMillan, Stranraer; Mrs J. Fergusson, Gatehouse; Mr J. Grieve, Gatehouse; Mr A. Curtis Wolffe, Gatehouse; Mr T. Raphael, Borgue; Mr J. Gordon, Kirkcudbright; Mrs I. Walker, Kirkcudbright; Mr D. Coulthard, Twynholm; Mr I. Galloway, Twynholm; Mr J. Henderson, Ringford; Mr N. McGill Duncan, Castle Douglas.

The publishers would like to thank Robert Grieves for providing the upper picture on page 4 and its accompanying caption, and Harry Jack who took the photograph on page 23.

FURTHER READING

In compiling this publication I have referred to many earlier works on the area, most of them out of print. The main ones are listed here while others are mentioned in the text. I am happy to acknowledge my indebtedness to all the authors whose books I have consulted. Please note that none of the following titles is available from Stenlake Publishing.

Anderson, A. D., *The Development of the Road System in the Stewartry* (TDGNHAS)
Donnachie, I., *The Industrial Archaeology of Galloway*
Elder, G., *Borgue: The Story of a Seaboard Parish*
Gifford, J., *The Buildings of Scotland: Dumfries and Galloway*
Macleod, I., *Discovering Galloway*
Mann, P., *The Gatehouse Experiment*
Pennell, W., *The Story of Knockbrex*
Russell, J., *The History of Education in the Stewartry of Kirkcudbright*
Smith, J., *Cheesemaking in Scotland: A History*
The Statistical Account of Scotland
The New Statistical Account of Scotland
The Third Statistical Account of Scotland

Dirk Hatteraick's Cave, Galloway's most famous smuggling location, is situated near Kirkdale Port but is difficult to find and equally difficult, indeed dangerous, to enter, since its floor is a good five metres below the level of the ground outside. It takes its name from the captain of the smuggling vessel in Scott's *Guy Mannering*, who was 'half Manks [i.e. Manx], half Dutchman, whole devil'. Much of the novel is set along this stretch of coastline. About fourteen metres long but nowhere more than two metres wide, the cave is, for the smuggler, extremely well-appointed with a wall built along one side with square pigeonholes, possibly for storing brandy bottles, and a natural hollow in the rock shaped like a ship's bunk. A water supply in the form of a stream and a crevice near the roof allegedly giving access to a second small cave – an ideal hiding place of last resort – complete its amenities.

INTRODUCTION

The part of Galloway comprising the former county of Kirkcudbright is still habitually described locally as the Stewartry. The origin of the name goes far back into Galloway history to a time when the lord of Galloway appointed a steward to administer his affairs in eastern Galloway. This duty was already carried out in west Galloway (Wigtownshire) by the hereditary royal sheriffs, the Agnews of Lochnaw. Whether the lord in question was Robert the Bruce, Archibald the Grim or James II depends on the authority consulted. The post was later made hereditary and bestowed on the Maxwells of Caerlaverock. The area administered by the steward was known as the stewardry or stewartry. For the purposes of this book the Central Stewartry is defined as the area lying between the Kirkdale Burn in the west and the River Tarff in the east.

Comprising coastal lowland and river valleys, this area is not only one of the most beautiful parts of Galloway but one of the most fertile. The pastoral nature of the agriculture means the landscape is predominantly green, diversified by frequent stands of hardwood trees, something sadly lacking in other parts of the province. The main type of farming is dairying and raising beef cattle, the latter including, but to a lesser extent than in the past, the various versions of the native Galloway breed.

Apart from beef and milk, the area is famed for another product of the land, honey. Specifically, this comes from the parish of Borgue, so renowned for the commodity that a favourite local tale relates that a shop or inn in London at one time was emblazoned with the sign 'Borgue honey for ever!'. It has been suggested that the quality of the celebrated honey derives from the short-stemmed clover which grows on the thin soil overlying the innumerable small, rocky hillocks or knowes for which the parish is noted.

While the main communities of the Central Stewartry, Borgue, Gatehouse, and Twynholm, have distinct characters, they also seem to possess two characteristics in common, although their residents might find this difficult to accept.

Firstly, in their present form all are comparatively modern with few if any buildings predating the eighteenth century. Yet the countryside close to them is studded with evidence of settlements from the distant past. Particularly frequent are the traces of hill- and promontory forts dating from the Iron Age 2,000 years ago. At least as common are mottes, artificial mounds of earth (now much eroded) in the shape of upturned pudding bowls. These formed the foundations of wooden castles built from the twelfth century on by Anglo–Norman nobles, brought in by a Scottish king anxious to pacify his unruly Galloway subjects. Of the abundant examples two of the most visible are the Doon of Twynholm, a fort on a tree-crowned hill west of the village, and nearby the spectacular motte at Boreland of Borgue. Gatehouse claims the distinction of having one of the few Roman sites discovered in Galloway, the fortlet north

of the village on the banks of the Fleet, visible only on aerial photographs.

The other characteristic shared by the three communities is significant literary associations. Borgue is almost certainly the real setting for the Scottish episodes in Robert Louis Stevenson's *The Master of Ballantrae*. The Stevenson family had a connection with the parish as RL's father was engineer in charge of the construction of the lighthouse on Little Ross island. Gatehouse has connections with Robert Burns and stronger ones with crime-writer Dorothy L. Sayers, whose *Five Red Herrings* is partly set in and around the village. Twynholm provided Sir Walter Scott with the prototype for his memorable character Wandering Willie in the novel *Redgauntlet*, but the story is a tragic one. In April 1816 a Welsh ex-soldier called Hugh Prichard, by that time blind, was passing through the parish on his return from Ireland accompanied by his wife and five children. They took shelter for the night in a gravel pit near the village and were all killed when the bank of the pit collapsed. Two headstones in the churchyard relate the grim events.

The coast of Central Galloway lacks good, natural harbours, something that was a disadvantage when coastal shipping was the main form of transport (but one which the ingenious entrepreneurs of Gatehouse overcame). Things did not improve when the emphasis shifted to land transport. The military road of 1763–64 linking Carlisle and Portpatrick avoided the coastal lowland between Gatehouse and Creetown. Instead it went through the moorland and hills to the north by way of Skyreburn Glen and the ferocious Corse of Slakes. Only in the late 1780s was the highway rerouted along the coast. The railway builders of 1858 followed the example of their military forebears but on a larger scale. Their line avoided the coastal lowlands of the Central Stewartry completely, once again taking to the northern moors.

The smugglers of the late eighteenth and early nineteenth centuries had no complaints about transport links in the area. The numerous secluded small bays and inlets suited their nefarious purposes perfectly and, together with the proximity of the Isle of Man and its relaxed customs laws, made this coast a smuggling hot spot.

Others with no complaints on the same score should have been the inhabitants of Borgue parish in 1300. Their situation somewhat off the beaten track may have averted a visit from Edward I, Hammer of the Scots, and his army while neighbouring Twynholm and Gatehouse enjoyed that doubtful privilege. On the other hand, Borgue's position attracted visitors who took the sea road and the numerous place names ending in '-ton' reveal an Anglo–Saxon presence here 1,300 years ago. They were followed in the tenth century by the formidable Norsemen, who left their mark on the map with the names Borgue, Borness, and Senwick.

Thus the Central Stewartry past, like the landscape, is rich and varied and both amply reward a closer acquaintance.

Since the late 1960s when this photograph was taken, the road running by Cardoness Castle has been moved twice. At the time it passed very close to the castle, but was later realigned further away, and now both it and Gatehouse are totally bypassed by the new A75. This view shows VCS 391, the first of the brand new 49-seat Leyland Leopards in the fleet of Western SMT, who provided the main link through Gatehouse on the Dumfries to Stranraer trunk service which at this period took three hours forty minutes. This important service had been operated by the Caledonian Omnibus Company of Dumfries until its take-over in 1949 by Western SMT.

Cardoness or Bardarroch House (the latter being the name of the land on which it was built) became the laird's house for Cardoness estate after grim Cardoness Castle went out of use in 1697. The estate has been owned by some of Galloway's best-known families: the McCullochs, the Gordons, the Maxwells and the Hannays, the latter still being in possession as the Rainsford-Hannays. The original Cardoness House was built in 1721 by Colonel William Maxwell, who as a medical student in Holland in 1688 had joined the future King William's expeditionary force to Britain and became a firm favourite of the king, serving with him in Flanders and Ireland and later commanding the government forces in southern Scotland during the Jacobite rising of 1715. The house, which had Dutch features, was extended in 1826 and replaced in 1889 by the mansion shown here, which in turn was greatly reduced in size and altered in 1960.

While the McCullochs have long disappeared from Cardoness estate, a branch of the family still possesses neighbouring Ardwall estate, which came into its possession in 1587 when McCulloch of Cardoness granted a feu of Nether Ardwall to his cousin William McCulloch. In the succeeding 400 years the family's history has not been without incident. In 1680 David McCulloch had his life declared forfeit for his adherence to Presbyterianism. In the eighteenth century another of the family, a ship's surgeon, was killed in the Mediterranean when his vessel was boarded by Barbary pirates. As a baby, a McCulloch wife, daughter of the provost of Dumfries, was hurriedly removed from her father's house prior to its threatened burning by Prince Charlie's soldiers in 1745. The 1762 mansion house, enlarged in 1895, was built of whinstone quarried from the beach. It has been claimed as the most delightful house in Galloway partly because of its close proximity to both sea and woodland.

Today the clachan of Anwoth is a peaceful backwater, but in the seventeenth century it was home to one of the most controversial figures in Scotland. Samuel Rutherford, the parish minister, was a leading champion of the Presbyterian cause in its long struggle with the government and the Stuart kings. During his twelve years in Anwoth he spent two years in banishment in Aberdeen and had his book *Lex Rex* burned at Edinburgh cross by the public hangman. He also attained the highest office, being Regent of Humanity at Edinburgh University before coming to Anwoth and leaving the parish to become Professor of Divinity at St Andrews. His church at Anwoth was built in 1627, the year of his arrival, and closed in 1826 when a new building was erected close by. The mausoleum of the Maxwells of Cardoness in the right foreground rather obscures the roofless church of modest dimensions.

Rutherford's Church, Anworth

The probable late-fourteenth century date for the bell from Rutherford's church suggests that the latter was not the first religious building on the site – or that the bell came from somewhere else. The inscription 'MARIA' on it suggests the latter. Its small size (the diameter at the mouth is only eleven inches) would not be a disadvantage as Rutherford's congregation needed no reminder or exhortation to attend church. In spite of a somewhat screeching voice he was a superb preacher, whose services were always packed. Another reason for his popularity was that in his personal relations he was kindly, affectionate and sympathetic, traits revealed in his famous letters. These are such outstanding examples of Christian teaching that they have rarely been out of print in the 350 years since they were written. But there was a less attractive side to his personality: in public matters, even within the Church of Scotland, he was disputatious, bitter, and implacable.

Anwoth old churchyard contains the grave of Covenanter John Bell of nearby Whiteside, who after several years as a fugitive for his Presbyterian sympathies was captured along with four companions in February 1685 on Kirkconnel Moor north of Ringford. Being the stepson of Viscount Kenmure and married to a McCulloch of Ardwall did nothing to save him from the summary justice of the time. On discovering that he and his friends were to be shot forthwith, he begged his captor, the formidable Grierson of Lag, for a short time for prayer. Grierson's uncompromising response was to suggest that Bell's seven years as a fugitive had afforded him ample time for that activity, and the prisoners were executed without more ado. They are commemorated by a monument on Kirkconnel Moor.

The aspiring industrial town of Gatehouse was handicapped by poor sea communications, since the meandering River Fleet made navigation between estuary and the harbour at Boat Green difficult. The problem was solved by the decision of Murray of Cally in 1824 to build a canal, and a remarkably ingenious piece of civil engineering by his factor, Alexander Craig. An expert estimate of £5,000 for the necessary work was confounded by two measures. Two hundred tenants from Murray's Donegal estate, in arrears of rent, were brought to Gatehouse to build the canal, their labour being taken as rent payment. Craig had them dig a narrow trench along the centre of the line of the proposed canal and diverted the waters of the river into it. In two days nature had excavated the canal to the required depth and width and all works were complete in under four months at a cost of £2,200. The Fleet Canal is almost a mile long and allowed ships of 160 tons to sail to the outskirts of Gatehouse.

The Fleet Canal stopped a quarter of a mile before the harbour at Boat Green, of which only the name remains. The intervening stretch of unimproved river was winding, but this drawback was eliminated in 1836–37 when a local merchant and ship owner, David McAdam, was given permission by laird Alexander Murray to construct a new harbour at the northern end of the canal. To compensate him, McAdam was given the right to levy landing charges; understandably he named the new facility after himself. At first the venture prospered with 99 vessels calling in 1846, but the coming of the steamship and the railway sounded the death knell for Galloway's smaller harbours, including Port McAdam. It continued to be used by coal boats until 1930 but then fell into disuse until 1974, when it was brought back into operation for small pleasure craft. This phase effectively ended in 1985 with the construction of the bypass bridge with its severely restricted headroom for canal users.

Port McAdam

By a happy accident, when the Fleet Canal was excavated two rocks were revealed at Cardoness Castle, one on each bank and exactly opposite each other. They were used as the bases of the pillars of a swing bridge, which brought the laird of Cally two advantages. The bridge improved access between his estate and the main Dumfries–Stranraer road, which now ran by Cardoness Castle and along the coast. It also allowed him to divert the local road from Gatehouse to the popular beach at Sandgreen across the new bridge and thus away from the immediate vicinity of his residence at Cally House. From now on the horse-drawn charabancs bound for the seaside took this route and Murray's privacy was restored. Today only the granite pillars of the bridge remain; everything else, including keeper's cottage and copse behind, has disappeared.

Gatehouse of Fleet.

33156. J.V.

The key element in James Murray's plans for an industrial town on the banks of the Fleet was the provision of motive power; in the late eighteenth century this meant water power. The source was Loch Whinyeon four miles north-east of Gatehouse, whence the water was brought by a series of lades and a tunnel to be stored in two reservoirs at the east end of the village, one on each side of the main road. From those the water was made available to potential users through two lades, one running on each side of the main highway and behind the houses in High Street. The southern reservoir (on the left) has been drained, but the northern one (right) survives, as does a considerable portion of the lade which it supplied. The large building in the centre of the picture, the four-storey Birtwhistle mill, now the Mill on the Fleet centre, was the principal beneficiary of Murray's scheme. Others benefiting were a further three cotton mills, a tannery, a brewery, and a brass foundry.

The name of the Anwoth Hotel is a reminder that the western part of Gatehouse lies in Anwoth parish, while the eastern part is in Girthon parish with the River Fleet, just out of the picture on the right, forming the boundary. The older name of the hotel, the Ship Inn, is equally appropriate for many of its patrons once came from the nearby harbour of Boat Green, which was also the site of a yard where boats were built and repaired. The Anwoth has claims to literary fame since Dorothy L. Sayers addressed the foreword of her famous whodunnit *The Five Red Herrings* to its owner Joe Dignam, 'kindliest of landlords' (and praised his wife's potato scones!). When she first came to Galloway, Sayers stayed at the hotel before buying a house in Kirkcudbright. The petrol pump at the corner, one of several in the village, is a reminder that petrol outlets were once much more numerous, if less well appointed, than today.

Fleetside School, 100 yards up the Dromore or Station Road from the Anwoth Hotel, owes its existence to the old Scottish principle of a school in every parish. Anwoth went one better with two schools, one at Laggan (later moved to Skyreburn) and one at Anwoth clachan. In 1872 the latter closed and a new school, Fleetside, opened in the largest population centre in the parish. It was housed in an enlarged building which had previously accommodated the Bland Female School; a sandstone plaque inscribed 'The Bland Female School, erected 1866' is built into a wall close to the entrance to the modern school. In 1923 Fleetside amalgamated with the Girthon parish school at the other end of the village and four years later the two schools were brought together in an again enlarged building at Fleetside, denominated Gatehouse School. Today the oldest part of the former Fleetside School, much altered from the photograph, is part of the community centre.

On the left is the former industrial heart of Gatehouse, the complex of three cotton mills, two of them built by the Yorkshire firm of Messrs Birtwhistle & Sons. The largest mill, roofless on the left, employed around 300 workers in its heyday at the end of the eighteenth century, over half of them children. After the closure of the cotton mills in the mid-nineteenth century, this building was converted to a bobbin mill supplying those essential items to more successful cotton mills nationwide until the early 1930s. In the centre stands the former Anwoth and Girthon United Free Church, diplomatically sited as close as possible to the boundary between those two parishes. On the right stands the bridge over the Fleet, built on the site of an older structure dating back to the early seventeenth century. This was rebuilt in 1661, but today's bridge is a much altered version of the 1730 model, the structure in the picture having been itself widened in 1965.

Across the Fleet and into Girthon parish, the building which gives Brewery Brae its name is inconveniently hidden by the trees in the left background. The brewery was established in 1784 by James Murray, who was anxious to create an outlet for local barley. The new enterprise certainly found a ready market for its products: a late eighteenth century traveller commented with astonished disapproval on the consumption of alcoholic beverages in Gatehouse. The collective thirst was also catered for by a small brewery in Ann Street and a wine company. Just visible directly across the road from the brewery is a white building, the subject of some controversy. Now a shop and restaurant complex, it is traditionally regarded as having originally been one of the village's two tanneries. However, the RIAS architectural guide suggests that its location and shape indicate it may have been the stables and coach house for the adjacent Angel Hotel.

HIGH STREET LOOKING NORTH WEST,
GATEHOUSE OF FLEET

Copyright
Ghe. 66

Although the Angel Hotel was built around 1800, its name suggests an earlier inn may have stood on this site, for inns with religious names often stood on pilgrim routes – in this case the way to the shrine of St Ninian at Whithorn. C. H. Dick, author of the classic *Highways and Byways in Galloway and Carrick*, preferred to stay at the Angel because of the fine view from the top storey rooms. In the left background, at the east end of High Street, can be seen the village's most distinctive building, the clock tower. In the right middleground, set back from the line of houses, the top of the gable of the town hall is just visible. It was completed in 1885 at a cost of £1,000, the sum being raised by public subscription, and housed a large painting by local artist John Faed. Amid much dispute the building was drastically 'downsized' in 1994 and today consists of little more than the facade.

The clock tower legitimately occupies centre stage in this view of the High Street from the east. In the Murray Arms, on the left, Burns may have committed *Scots Wha Hae* to paper after composing it on the journey from Laurieston in a thunderstorm. The awning on the right marks the position of the building which served for many years as Hendersons' grocery store. In the 1920s Norah Henderson struck an early blow for equal opportunities by driving the firm's motor van on its rounds. Hendersons' successors in the shop were the local co-operative society. The genesis of the clock tower was the gift of £30 by local man Andrew Finlay in 1867 for the purpose of erecting a public clock. In the following four years the sum increased tenfold by subscriptions and a tower of Craignair granite was erected to house the projected clock, which was donated by Mr Murray Stewart of Cally.

The mild climate claimed by the guidebooks for Gatehouse is not in evidence here, the residents' dress suggesting a date around 1900 for the unusual event. Behind the window advertising Raleigh cycles the McMurray family ran an ironmonger's and watchmaker's business for many years. Beside them, on the right, the present-day butcher's was formerly a shoe shop, owned first by Mr Johnstone and then Mr Riddick. Three doors down, adjacent to the gas lamp, the Stark family operated a chemist's business for generations. Another two doors down, the building that is now Galloway Lodge used to be two separate units, one occupied by Mr Tait the painter, and the other by barber Mr McNeillie. The gas for the street lamps came from the gasworks at the western end of the village. Its chimney is visible in the pictures on pages 10 and 12 and the site, later occupied by a garage, is now the location of Fleet Valley Nursing Home.

Catherine Street, Gatehouse-of-Fleet

In this view Catherine Street still retains a mill town quality consistent with Gatehouse's industrial past. C. H. Dick commented on this feature of the village as late as 1916. James Murray laid out his planned village in the 1760s in imitation of Edinburgh's New Town in a grid with three main streets, High Street, Catherine Street and Birtwhistle Street, the eastward curve of the River Fleet foreshortening the last two. Houses in High Street had to be two storeys high and have slate roofs; in the other two streets they were permitted to be 'meaner' in their structure and dimensions but were to be 'equally orderly in their arrangements'.

Gatehouse acquired the services of a Roman Catholic priest in 1800, when Fr Andrew Carruthers, newly appointed chaplain to Maxwell of Munches, extended his duties to minister to the surrounding area. Later the village became the responsibility of the Dalbeattie priest and arrangements were probably the same as at nearby Kirkcudbright, where mass was celebrated in a hired room every two months. By 1843 the Gatehouse congregation was around 150 strong. The appointment of a resident priest to Kirkcudbright in the late nineteenth century permitted weekly masses at Gatehouse and by the early twentieth century the congregation had acquired its own property, shown here, at 10 Catherine Street. The ground floor was let as a dwelling house while the first floor served as St Mary's Roman Catholic Chapel. The building was sold around 1971 and the congregation moved to a purpose-built chapel, the Church of the Resurrection, in Riverbank.

Until 1820 the highway from Carlisle to Portpatrick entered Gatehouse by way of Ann Street (illustrated here) before turning down towards the bridge. Before James Murray started to lay out his new village in the 1760s the only house that stood on the site was the one gable-on to the street in the centre of the picture known as the 'gait house', the house on the gait or road. The replacement or extension of this inn by the Murray Arms on its left was the first step in the development of modern Gatehouse. The first floor of the Masonic Arms, on the right, was the hall of the local Freemasons, Masonic Lodge St Stephen's, from 1785. Access was by the door in the darker-coloured wing on the left. A scene from Scott's *Guy Mannering* is supposedly set in the Masonic Arms.

The unveiling and dedication of the war memorial for the parishes of Anwoth and Girthon in 1921. The monument, at the east end of Gatehouse High Street, is a Celtic cross of Creetown granite. At its unveiling there were 88 names on it, a number that was increased by fourteen as a result of the Second World War. Behind the memorial is the northerly of the two reservoirs serving the lades, and in the left foreground the bowed end of the former tollhouse. This was built around 1820 after a realignment of the toll road on the eastern outskirts of Gatehouse. It replaced three earlier versions in Ann Street on the former line of the turnpike. An Act of Parliament of 1797 had authorised the construction in the Stewartry of turnpikes or toll roads, an idea whose time seems to have come again. The act decreed a minimum distance of six miles between toll bars. Today the building is the headquarters of a firm of architects.

The Golf Course, Gatehouse

GHE 6.

LILYWHITE.LTD.
TRIANGLE.H.X.

A short distance up the Laurieston road from the war memorial lies Gatehouse golf course, described in guides of 50 years ago as 'a sporting 9-hole course'. The terrain visible in the picture certainly seems to justify the epithet. That or perhaps the extension in length of 30 yards may explain why the par 33 of the 1940s became the 35 of the 1950s. Sunday golf was permitted in the late 1940s, a fairly radical concession. The club may not always have had its course here: a 1908 publication refers to a 9-hole course in Cally Park, the policies of Cally House. While the clubhouse is little changed externally, the house in the foreground has acquired two dormer windows. A hundred metres further up the road to the left is Barlay Mill, birthplace of the Faed family of extraordinary artistic talent, three of whom achieved national renown – John and Tom as painters and James as an engraver.

This rear view of Rusco (Rusko) House, just over a mile from Gatehouse up the station road, also features the region's famous Belted Galloway cattle, fittingly enough as Anwoth parish was the home of some of their most notable breeders. The original house with its hipped roof and semicircular projection at the back is discernible, hemmed in between the later wings on either side. The successor to Rusco Castle as the residence of the laird of Rusco estate, it was probably built by Robert Hannay of Jamaica when he purchased the estate in 1800. The extensions may well have followed the sale of the lands in 1879 to Mr H. Murray Stewart of Cally for £40,000. Mr Murray Stewart had sold his estate of Killybegs in Ireland and was anxious to reinvest the proceeds in land nearer his main property. Rusco, which means 'marshy land' in Gaelic, was also known in earlier times as Skyreburn or Glenskyreburn.

Rusco Castle or tower house was built around 1500 as the laird's residence for Rusco estate. The estate's first owners, the Carsons or Acarsons, were succeeded by the Gordons of Lochinvar, the McGuffocks from Wigtownshire, and the Hannays. During the 200 years of Gordon ownership one Gordon wife played the role of Agatha Christie's Miss Marple in frustrating the evil designs of her husband's grieve, Peter Carnochan. The latter devised a plan to ruin Andrew Dennistoun, his successful rival for the hand of local beauty Barbara Bell, by framing him for sheep stealing, a capital offence. Lady Gordon's sharp eyes and quick wits frustrated the scheme at the eleventh hour, Carnochan dangled from a rope, and Dennistoun took his place as grieve. After Rusco House was built the castle was used as a shooting lodge, then servants' quarters, before being finally abandoned in the early twentieth century. Between 1975 and 1979 it was restored by the present owner, Mr R. G. Carson.

When the Castle Douglas to Portpatrick railway was built no station was planned for Gatehouse, but that decision was reversed after public pressure. The station had three claims to fame: at 495 feet it was the summit of the eventual Dumfries to Stranraer line; it was further away from the community it served (six miles) than any other station in Britain; and it was the only station on the line to have its name changed – from Dromore to Gatehouse. So inaccessible was its situation that substantial road improvements and a stretch of new road were required to link it with the village, originally by horse-drawn coach. Closed in 1949, it was reopened after community pressure and remained so until the line finally shut down in 1965. Tragedy marked its early days when on the evening of New Year's Day, 1863, stationmaster John Alexander, walking back along the line after visiting friends in Creetown, was hit by a train and fatally injured.

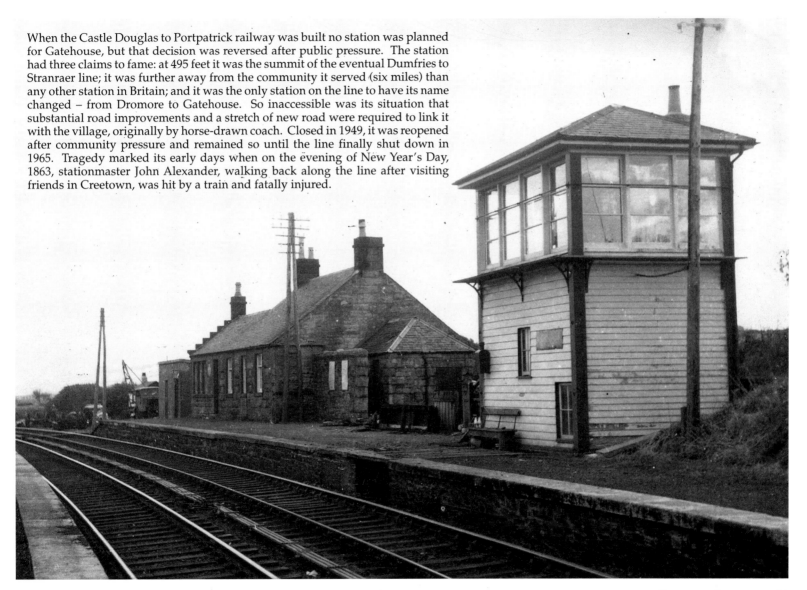

Built of granite from the immediate neighbourhood, the Big Water of Fleet viaduct a mile east of Gatehouse station was one of the best-known features of the Dumfries to Stranraer line and remains a prominent landmark. It has 20 arches and a maximum height of 70 feet. Problems with the structure led to major repairs in 1912 while a long-term project to encase all the piers in brickwork lasted eighteen years. Just before completion of the original viaduct in September 1860, a boy working on a crane had an astonishing escape when he attempted to return to the ground by jumping into a descending bucket instead of using the ladder. Despite a fall of 80 feet his only injuries were two broken ribs. The firm which built the Big Water of Fleet structure also built the viaducts at Loch Ken and Glenluce.

LOCH SKERROW, NEAR GATEHOUSE-OF-FLEET.

Remote Loch Skerrow was formerly noted as a source of pearls as well as sand for sharpening scythes, and is still celebrated for the size and quality of its trout. No road to it existed until the Forestry Commission built one in the mid-1950s. Surprisingly, however, it was accessible by rail for a halt was built there to allow steam engines to take on water. This necessitated the presence of personnel, houses for their accommodation, and wooden platforms to allow wives and children to travel by train to shops and school. Although Loch Skerrow did not appear on railway timetables until 1955, for nearly 100 years previously anglers – and curlers – had journeyed there by train with official approval and after signing a form absolving the rail company of any responsibility for their fate. Railway families supplemented their income by providing board and lodging for the visitors and acting as boatmen for the fishers.

Bush Bridge is situated in the former policies of Cally House a short way in from the entrance lodges and east of the road leading to the modern hotel. A stone-built, single-arched structure, it carried the Carlisle to Portpatrick highway into Gatehouse via Ann Street until 1820. In that year laird Murray of Cally had the line of the main road moved northward to take it further away from his mansion. To effect this he had a cutting made through the ominously named Gallow Hill at a cost to him of £3,000. This stretch of road is still known as the Cut. The purpose of the wooden footbridge under the arch of the bridge is not obvious. It has long disappeared but the sockets in the stonework for the beams that carried it are still visible.

In the 1760s James Murray of Broughton and Cally had a new mansion built for himself half a mile south of his existing residence outside Gatehouse. Perhaps his mother's and wife's connection with the Earls of Galloway stimulated his ambitions. In this he followed his father, who had had plans for a new house drawn up by the celebrated William Adam; however only the pavilions flanking the main block were built, to be demolished later. Son James was more successful: the design by Robert Mylne was duly turned into dressed blocks of Kirkmabreck granite, the first time this method of construction had been used in southern Scotland. Seventy-five years later the mansion was made even grander by the addition of a portico with granite pillars, quarried at Craigdews near Clatteringshaws, and a marble lobby. The furnishings matched the splendour of the building with paintings by Velasquez, Durer and Reynolds. James Murray also built Broughton House in Kirkcudbright's High Street as the family's town residence.

The rear view of Cally House shows the chapel on the extreme left, partly hidden by the monkey puzzle tree. Built in 1857, it was demolished in 1990. It was the organist at Cally, George Hornsby, who wrote the music for the region's national anthem, *Bonnie Gallowa'*, the words being the work of local farmer and poet George G. B. Sproat. The Murrays of Broughton near Whithorn came into possession of the Cally estate around 1655 when Richard Murray married its Lennox heiress, and it remains in their ownership. However the house and policies were taken over in 1933 by the Forestry Commission, who then sold the building to a Fort William hotelier for £2,000. His ownership of the Palace Hotel in that town led him to name his new venture the Cally Palace Hotel. Apart from during the Second World War, when the house became a residential secondary school for evacuee children from Glasgow, Cally has been a hotel since that time under a variety of owners.

THE HUT, GATEHOUSE OF FLEET

CARRICK, GATEHOUSE OF FLEET.

In his account of Galloway in 1692 Andrew Symson remarked, 'Our sea is better stored with good fish, than our shoare is furnished with good fishers'. His comments certainly were not true of the estate fishery at Carrick on the east side of Fleet Bay in the twentieth century, where manager Mr Davidson ran a very successful operation first on behalf of the estate and then on his own account. He appears on the right of the left-hand photograph accompanied by two of his family of ten children. Also featured in the photograph is the essential equipment for the stake net fishery, but despite the illustration being captioned 'The Hut' that building is not visible in the picture. Made of wood, it was the residence of the fishery manager. Salmon were caught in season and white fish at other times. The more substantial building in the right-hand photograph with a cow seeking admission was situated nearby and occupied by the grieve on Carrick farm.

The start of a sailing race in Fleet Bay, the starter poised with his gun on the right. The distinctive profile of the hills in the background reveals the event is taking place on the east shore, and the rocky foreshore suggests the location is Carrick rather than the appropriately named Sandgreen (the latter was the usual centre of seaside leisure activities). While formal racing was not frequent, Fleet Bay was a popular sailing location. Gatehouse draper Mr Fergusson often brought his boat down from Port McAdam while the Carr family of the well-known Carlisle biscuit-manufacturing firm occasionally called in their cruising yacht. Carrick was popular with local artists as well as sailing enthusiasts. David Sassoon did much of his painting there while T. McGill Duncan and W. Miles Johnstone had huts on the site. E. A. Hornel arrived to paint in chauffeur-driven style while on Sundays Cecile Walton and Dorothy Johnstone came by more modest transport for the same purpose.

KNOCKBREX, KIRKCUDBRIGHT.

Knockbrex House, down the coast from Carrick, was built in 1900 by Manchester businessman James Brown, who had bought the estate six years before. It incorporates an earlier house, just out of the picture on the right. Although Brown bought Knockbrex from the Earl of Selkirk, the family most closely associated with the property were a branch of the Gordons of Lochinvar. Staunch Presbyterians in the long religious struggles in Scotland in the seventeenth century, they suffered grievously for their loyalty. Two Gordon sons were captured fighting for the Covenanting forces in the Pentland Rising of 1666 and executed together. Twenty years later 200 of the locust-like Highland Host were billeted at Knockbrex to punish the Gordons and left the house plundered and badly damaged. A second plundering was under the command of no less than Grierson of Lag. At the start of the nineteenth century the house's stabling for 70 horses indicated a deep involvement in the locally thriving smuggling trade.

AT KNOCKBREX. SEPTEMBER. 11TH 1913.

The younger members of the company dance the afternoon away to the music of the quadrille band from Kirkcudbright at a garden party for Stewartry Liberals at Knockbrex House in September 1913. The Browns were active Liberal supporters. With the constituency regained at the previous general election and a Liberal government in power, spirits were high. Other activities on offer included croquet, a coconut shy, and an Aunt Sally stall. The less active could stroll in the water garden, rock garden, or Knockbrex's famous rose garden. Tea in the marquee on the left was enormously popular: at one point over 500 guests were seated within. However, the event had its formal side; at the end of the afternoon the company of 900 assembled on the 'seaward lawn' to be addressed from the balcony by the VIP guests, Lord and Lady Haddo. His lordship had previously caused a stir by mingling with the throng in full Highland regalia.

James Brown of Knockbrex's enthusiasm for a highly imaginative and uninhibited style of architecture with echoes of the medieval might almost earn him the title of Galloway's Antonio Gaudi and cause Borgue parish to be equated with Barcelona. Its most spectacular expression is the Corseyard model dairy near Kirkandrews. The byre itself is in the form of a nave with side aisles, the whole tiled within and equipped with solid brass tethering chains and drinking bowls. The turreted, battlemented tower was intended as a water tower but later converted to a grain silo. Those in search of further exotic delights should seek out the tool shed, a miniature round tower, or the keyhole-shaped gateway to the vegetable garden. On the shore nearby an Iron Age fort, Castle Haven, of a type unusual in Galloway, also received the Brown treatment, somewhat to the consternation of the relevant authorities. Having excavated it, the laird had the drystone walls rebuilt to most of their postulated original height.

The Model Dairy, Corseyard, Borgue.

Kirkandrews Hall, Borgue.

This frowning fortress in Kirkandrews village is another James Brown creation. Despite its turret, battlements and portcullis it is, in fact, the village hall, opened in 1908, which he generously put at the service of the people of the parish for any meeting of a religious, social, or political kind. Part of the elaborate wooden lych-gate with its red-tiled roof is visible on the right; the tower above the door houses a bell, and the little turret on the left is the chimney for a large open fireplace. Always popular for weddings, the building is now used mainly for ecumenical church services and is owned by a trust. Not everyone was impressed by James Brown's architectural initiatives. A writer in the 1950s complained, 'There seems to be nothing but castles here . . . The whole place is a medley of battlements'. In fact one of the delights of the area is the less obtrusive details of stonework: walls, paved areas, stiles.

The clachan of Kirkandrews or Kirkanders stands on an inlet of the Solway where the Pulwhirrin and Burnyard Burns meet and flow into the sea. Until the late twelfth century the church here belonged to the monks of Iona, suggesting that the place may be named not after Scotland's patron saint but after a ninth century Irish saint of the same name. The clachan was in the seventeenth century the venue for horse and foot races and famous for its annual St Lawrence's fair, held in the churchyard on the 9th of August. Although the event lasted, mercifully, only a few hours, 'the people, who resorted thither in great numbers, enjoyed in the meantime all the debauch of a rude age'. No pier existed but it was recorded around 1800 that small vessels could anchor in the bay in good weather. Despite the lack of landing facilities Kirkandrews was much used by smugglers and the suppression of that activity in the early nineteenth century gravely affected its economy.

These thatched cottages formed part of the clachan of Kirkandrews and may have been occupied by fishermen, since a little of that activity was carried on. However, an attempt to set up a stake net fishery in the early nineteenth century was unsuccessful. In his *Rambles in Galloway* in 1896 Castle Douglas banker Malcolm Harper mourned the passing of several of 'these picturesque cottages under the exacting regulations of the Local Government act as to sanitary and other arrangements'. He also claimed that Gatehouse artist Thomas Faed had used one of the interiors as the setting for a well known painting. Close by in the churchyard are the remains of the medieval church, and the churchyard also houses the grave of local poet William Nicholson, author of the magnificent work with its roots deep in folklore *The Brownie o Blednoch*.

On the left stand the replacements for the Kirkandrews thatched cottages whose disappearance was so lamented by Malcolm Harper, if not by their occupants. Just to the right of centre is the village hall, while below and to its right the other battlemented building is the public wash house, another amenity provided in unconventional guise by James Brown and now, in much extended form, a private dwelling. But the clachan was famous for its residents as well as its buildings. In the religious strife of the seventeenth century Andrew Sword, weaver of Kirkandrews, was captured while fighting with the Covenanting forces at Bothwell Bridge in 1679. After imprisonment in the open air in Edinburgh's Greyfriars churchyard he was offered his liberty but on conditions which would have compromised his principles. His immediate rejection of the offer was followed by his execution, but not before he had sorely tried his captors' patience by insisting on singing all 22 verses of the 25th Psalm before the hangman could go about his business.

Joiner and wheelwright William Walker in contemplative mood outside his workshop at Ivy Cottage a mile west of Borgue. The light cart behind him emphasises his key role in the rural community as maker and mender of wooden wheels for horse-drawn carts, a complex and highly skilled craft. The wooden gate on the right reflects his innovative skills since it is probably part of a cattle crush which he invented. Essentially a narrow pen, it was designed to hold a cow or bullock while it received veterinary or other close attention. Another of William Walker's inventions showed his ability to adapt to the times. He designed and made one of the earliest pneumatic-tyred trailers for use with tractors and other vehicles, and his Borgue Trailer proved very popular with local farmers. The fishing rod on his right indicates one of his leisure interests. The other was bee-keeping: he was a leading apiarist in a parish famed for its honey.

William Walker's light-coloured house and workshop are visible facing the camera in the centre of this picture. Although the postcard is captioned 'Chapelton Row', the Row is actually out of sight at the foot of the hill beyond the row of houses in the middleground. These are associated with the smithy on the left, where blacksmith Willie Moffat fitted the iron tires to Walker's cartwheels. As another joiner, William McVitie, practised his trade in Chapelton Row, this area could perhaps be called Borgue's industrial suburb. Chapelton Row was so called because it stood at the end of the road leading to the farm of that name, a name which indicates the presence of a religious house in the vicinity in the remote past. It has been suggested that this was established and serviced by the monks from Kirkandrews. The house in the right foreground enjoys a magnificent view of Wigtown Bay and the Solway Firth beyond.

Only the small hayricks in the foreground and the size of the churchyard show that this is a scene from the past. In fact, a church has stood here since the early twelfth century when Sir Hugo de Morville, Constable of Scotland, erected the first building; the present church dates from 1814. Because of its commanding position Borgue parish church was often known as 'the visible kirk'. One of its best known ministers is the Revd Samuel Smith, who in the early nineteenth century wrote the classic *A General View of the Agriculture of Galloway*. In the churchyard is a memorial stone to Borgue native John Wilson, who served in the 17th Lancers and fell in the Charge of the Light Brigade at the Battle of Balaclava during the Crimean War.

BORGUE VILLAGE NEAR KIRKCUDBRIGHT.   223427.J.V.

Borgue village is dominated by the Borgue Hotel in the centre of the picture. For 80 years until the 1970s the name was something of a misnomer since the sale of alcohol was not permitted in the parish, hence the establishment's other name, 'The Coffee House'. The public hall in the right foreground was erected in 1932 as a result of community fund-raising, and opened by celebrated Scottish entertainer Sir Harry Lauder. On the other side of the road the pumps indicate the location of Rogerson's garage, workplace of the legendary Jimmy Raphael. Across from the village hall a plaque above the door marks the tearoom run by the two Misses Clark, who also provided accommodation. Just out of sight on the right is the famous Soup Kitchen, where by voluntary effort inexpensive but nourishing meals were provided for the children of Borgue school (on the left beyond the hotel) for 70 years until the advent of the school meals service.

Borgue Academy is one of the most famous schools in Galloway. It was founded in the eighteenth century by Thomas Rainy, a native of the parish, who had emigrated to the island of Dominica and made a fortune. A boarding establishment, its fame was such that boys were sent from long distances to study there. A further bequest by John Brown of Knockmulloch allowed the school to become co-educational. The plaque on the right-hand wall of the building commemorated Rainy until erosion erased its inscription. The monument on the low wall beside the road celebrates local poet William Nicholson. Today's building, still the local school, is much changed: the headmaster's house, gable-on to the road, and including accommodation for boarders, has been removed. The cottages on the right, belonging to Borgue House estate, were extensively renovated in 1931 and given red-tiled roofs and half-timbered porches. On the left is the strategically situated sweet shop latterly owned by Mary Ellen McHarg.

Earlstoun House, north-west of Borgue, was built around 1850 as the mansion for the estate previously known as Carleton. When that estate was inherited in 1816 by one of the famous Gordon family formerly of Earlstoun near Dalry in the Glenkens, its name was changed to that of the family's old home, and the new house similarly designated. The most famous resident of Borgue's Earlstoun House was Sir William Gordon. As a captain in the 17th Lancers he took part in the Charge of the Light Brigade at Balaclava, receiving several wounds. It is likely that John Wilson of Borgue, who fell in the Charge, had joined the 17th Lancers at the instigation of Sir William, for at that time officers were expected personally to recruit the members of their detachment. Sir William's charger was more fortunate than John Wilson, surviving the battle to return to Borgue and eventually be buried in the grounds of Earlstoun. The house is now demolished.

The view across the head of Brighouse Bay near Borgue, looking west. Like neighbouring Kirkandrews Bay, Brighouse was described in 1793 as being used by small ships in fine weather. Unlike Kirkandrews, however, Brighouse Bay boasts a jetty, stone-built and constructed in the nineteenth century. It is just visible in the centre. Brighouse was also popular with smugglers. A nineteenth century resident of the parish, Sproat of Millha', reminisced regretfully of the days that saw 'Tam MacMinn and me coupin ower a dizzen bumpers o' strong Holland gin (rare smuggled stuff) down at the Brighouse Bay o' a forenicht'. The bay was also frequented by Kirkcudbright artist E. A. Hornel, who used it as the backcloth for paintings like *Blue Flax* and *Sea Shore Roses*. One wonders what old Milha' would have made of the holiday complex and the terminal for the submarine gas pipeline to the Irish Republic, both now to be found on the shores of Brighouse bay.

The cyclists are resting at the foot of the burn that runs down to the Dee estuary from the cottage shown on the front cover. Many people have lingered here for this is the south end of the Doon, a highly popular beach between Borgue and Kirkcudbright. In the left foreground can be seen one of its best known features, the hulk of the schooner *Monreith*, wrecked here in November 1900. Built at Port William, the ship was on passage from Newcastle, County Down, to Silloth in Cumberland with a load of granite kerbstones when she came to grief. Luckily there were no casualties, the crew succeeding in getting ashore in the ship's boat before the lifeboat arrived from the other side of the estuary. Much more of the *Monreith* survives in the picture than is the case today. Beyond the cottages Senwick Wood runs for several miles down the side of the bay; this was another favourite setting for E. A. Hornel's paintings.

DOON BAY, KIRKCUDBRIGHT.

A 8540

The view across the Doon bay up the estuary towards Kirkcudbright makes clear the reasons for the beach's popularity. In the foreground is a gamekeeper's cottage on Senwick estate. In its early days the latter had two owners with royal connections, John Baliol, father of the unfortunate king of the same name; and Isabel, Countess of Athole and sister of Robert the Bruce. The heavily wooded bank in the left background conceals evidence of much earlier human inhabitants of the area: a 2,000-year old fort at the top of a steep bank. With a horseshoe shape, it is defended by two formidable ramparts of earth and stone alternating with two ditches. This large and impressive structure, well preserved in places, commanded the estuary. Sadly the dense woodland makes it impossible to see from any distance and difficult to visit. It gives its name to the shore below, 'dun' in Gaelic meaning a fort.

The names Nunmill, High Nunton and Lower Nunton in the vicinity of the Doon reflect the former existence of a nunnery in the area. The round-headed arch in the stretch of old wall in the left middleground, just north of the Doon shore, may well mark its site. The nunnery was of the Cistercian type, dedicated to St Evoca, and founded in the early fifteenth century. The building on the right, now a house, is a former corn mill on the Corraford Burn. At this point a minor road from Twynholm joins the coast road. It was built by Lord Daer, eldest son and heir to the Earl of Selkirk, to give access from the interior to the 'safe and commodious' harbour at Balmangan or Ross Bay a few miles further down the coast. The Female School, situated in the second building from the left, was also the work of the Selkirk family. Apart from building and maintaining it, members of the family showed their interest by frequent visits.

The street plan of Twynholm is complex since the Carlisle–Portpatrick highway has followed three different routes through it, with ribbon development on each. This view down Mill Brae (now Captain's Brae) shows some of the oldest part of the village, built on and near the military road of 1763–64, which crossed the Auchengassel or Kirk Burn by a bridge built in 1740 by the kirk session. The rear of the mill occupies the left middleground. Six years later the line of the highway was substantially altered to run in a southerly loop from Rhonehouse via Tongland and Cumstoun, before approaching Twynholm from the south along the high ground in the background and rejoining the previous line at the church, top right. The latter, built in 1818, is the latest in a series of churches built on or near the same site and dating back to 1200. The churchyard contains a memorial to two Twynholm residents who were lost in the notorious sinking of the liner *Lusitania* in 1915.

MILL BRAE, TWYNHOLM.

Twynholm woollen mill on the banks of the Auchengassel Burn (foreground). The wooden lade and overshot waterwheel have long gone, but the hole for the drive shaft is still in the mill wall. In the mid-nineteenth century both a woollen and a flax mill occupied the building, each used only by local farmers to produce cloth for their domestic needs. However, by the end of that century the building was owned by Mr Stewart, principal entrepreneur in the district, who manufactured successfully for a wider market. A 1901 advert for his 'Gallowa' ' hand-loom, home spun products 'in all the new and most fashionable shades and mixtures' offered wrap shawls, carriage rugs and gentlemen's mauds (plaids) plus suits, all at wholesale prices. His 'wareroom' at Castle Douglas, open on Mondays, was surely Galloway's first factory shop. William Stewart was a key member of the community, being also postmaster and chairman of the public hall trustees. His mill seems to have ceased production about 1910.

The main street in New Twynholm, looking east. The highway by Twynholm took yet another line after the 1797 Act of Parliament permitted the introduction of toll roads. This led to a virtually new road from Dumfries to Portpatrick, essentially the modern A75. At Twynholm the new toll- or mail coach road wound up the north side of the valley of the Auchengassel Burn to gain the high ground. The houses that grew up along it comprise New Twynholm, somewhat disparagingly referred to in an 1825 publication as 'a few straggling houses on the mail road'. This stretch of the way was, according to local tradition, built by French prisoners of war during the Napoleonic Wars. The large house in the centre of the picture was built by Wm. Payne. He owned the sawmill, originally powered by Twynholm's other burn, and the joinery business visible on the right beside the trees. The latter was later bought by the firm of J. & G. Brown & Sons. The complex is now demolished.

This stretch of Twynholm main street, its eastern end, lies immediately beyond the part shown in the picture above. The carts are parked outside Browns' wood store waiting for attention in the joinery shop across the road. The building on the right with the sign above the door is the Star Inn, now nationally renowned thanks to the exploits of local Formula 1 racing driver David Coulthard and to TV commentator Murray Walker ('They'll be celebrating in the Star Inn tonight'). The inn dates from 1913, when it was converted from a private house by Mr Sam Maxwell. In the centre of the picture is the village hall, built in 1896. It may have housed the recreation and reading rooms and carpet bowling club which the village boasted in 1901, when Twynholm also supported quoiting and curling clubs.

This shot of Twynholm main street looking west shows how the toll road wound up the hill in order to ease the gradient, a technique pioneered in this area by Lord Daer, an enthusiastic road builder and friend of Robert Burns, whom he entertained at St Mary's Isle, whence perhaps the famous *Selkirk Grace*. The house in the right middleground displays two lamp standards. The lower, older one would have held an oil lamp but the upper one is historically important for Twynholm claims to be the first village in Scotland to have had electric street lighting. In 1911, after the woollen mill had closed, owner Mr Stewart used the water wheel to power a generator which supplied electricity that illuminated not only the streets but also most of the houses. The stone magazine on the left, containing material for the road, shows that the latter did not yet enjoy a tarmacadam surface. Sadly it is not possible to identify the premises of the marvellously named mid-nineteenth century shoemaker James Leatherdale in this picture.

Tarff Creamery, a mile below Twynholm on the Twynholm Burn, was established in the late nineteenth century by the Valleyfield Dairy Company. In 1891 the latter amalgamated with the Dunragit Creamery Company to form United Creameries Ltd. Takeovers in 1938 and 1959 led to the creamery being owned by national firms United Dairies and then Unigate. In its early days Tarff made butter and cheese but in the difficult economic conditions of the 1920s and 1930s switched to processing whey from Kirkcudbright and Pinwherry creameries. The whey was dried in former wine presses, milled, and sold for paper making. In 1936 the total permanent workforce was thirteen. After World War II Tarff continued to specialise in processing whey from cheese-producing creameries in the area for eventual sale to the pharmaceutical and baking industries. It closed in the early 1970s after its major whey suppliers acquired their own processing equipment.

Sandwiched between a ford over a tributary of the River Tarff and an entrance to Queenshill House, the clachan of Ringford reveals its origins by its position. It was once known as the Red Lion after the inn where the mail coach horses were changed and travellers refreshed themselves. The inn in question is the two-storey building on the left nearest the camera. It closed in 1927, its last owner being a local builder, Mr Armour. Although it is now a private house, the inn sign is still stored there. The clachan also had a smithy until 1947, when Mr H. McGarva closed down. Even in 1952 it was well catered for with two grocery shops, one of them combined with the post office. The sign above the door of the last house on the right identifies the location of one of the shops. The entrance to Queenshill House was just round the corner in the trees.

Ringford from the opposite (east) end of the street. The last building on the left was the grocer's shop and post office. The three houses on the right beyond the railings of the village hall were built by Queenshill estate for their workers, emphasising the estate village character of Ringford. Around the mid-nineteenth century the estate was bought by James Beaumont Neilson, who revolutionised the iron industry by inventing the hot-blast method of smelting iron, which reduced the consumption of coal in the process by at least half. Chief engineer and manager of Glasgow Gasworks for 30 years, Neilson is commemorated by a prominent monument erected by his son on Bartstobrick Hill behind Ringford. It is pyramidal in shape and built of local whinstone. Queenshill House was destroyed by fire in the late nineteenth century. The village hall was erected by Neilson to serve as a form of adult education centre or mechanics' institute.

The New Mill, situated on the River Tarff a mile north of Ringford on the Laurieston road, was the estate sawmill for the Queenshill estate: cut, stacked timber can be seen just to the left of centre, while the waterwheel is to the right. The estate's original name of Culquha was changed to Queenshill about 1800 in deference to a local, erroneous tradition that Queen Mary in her flight to the Solway after her defeat at the Battle of Langside in 1568 paused briefly on a hill on the estate. While the date and circumstances of the supposed regal visit are incorrect, the visit itself almost certainly took place, but five years earlier. In August 1563, on a tour of Galloway, Mary travelled from Kenmure Castle to the priory of Traill on St Mary's Isle near Kirkcudbright. Her route took her down Loch Ken to the Tarff valley and so it is highly likely that the party rested just above Ringford, thus justifying the estate's amended name.

The building of Port McAdam (page 8) allowed larger vessels and bigger cargoes to gain access to Gatehouse: 2,600 tons of goods were landed in 1846. These mainly took the form of coal, agricultural fertilisers and feedstuffs. The firm of Belford was heavily involved in this trade. Like other concerns, it would have had a shed or warehouse at the harbour but it also had business premises in Digby Street, the commercial district of Gatehouse. Geographical considerations meant that most maritime trade was conducted across the Solway or the Irish Sea with Cumberland and Lancashire. This picture is reproduced from a rather tattered Belford's postcard addressed to a firm in Maryport acknowledging receipt of a cargo of potatoes and ordering a consignment of propwood (props for supporting cornstacks). Belford's eventually moved out of the agricultural requisites sector but operated as coal merchants for over 100 years, being still in business in 1965.

Back cover: The Brown family of Knockbrex (pages 30 and following) were noted breeders of the famed and photogenic Belted Galloway cattle. James Brown formed a herd in 1904 after abandoning plans to breed Galloway ponies because of shrinking demand. His 40-strong herd appeared in the first volume of the breed's Herd Book in 1921. After Mr Brown's death his widow took over management of the herd and was succeeded in that role in 1927 by her son, Mr J. Douglas Brown. He changed the herd prefix to 'Roberton' when he moved to that farm on the estate after selling Knockbrex House in 1945. After over 50 years' residence and numerous showring successes Belted Galloways finally disappeared from the former Knockbrex estate when the herd was sold at Castle Douglas in 1957. The average price obtained of £95 per animal was high for its day. Although Belted Galloways are kept for their beef, James Brown milked his for his own domestic use and ultimately had milk-recorded, tuberculin-tested animals, something of a novelty in the breed.

The CENTRAL STEWARTRY

Jack Hunter

With Compliments of the Season

"Belted Galloway's"

Knockbrex,

Kirkcudbright,

Published by:
**Stenlake Publishing,
54–58 Mill Square,
Catrine, Ayrshire KA5 6RD**
Telephone/fax: 01290 551122
www.stenlake.co.uk

Printed by:
**Cordfall Ltd
Glasgow G21 2QA**

£7.50

ISBN 1 84033 209 3

9 781840 332094